Also by Pamela Sackett

Two Minutes To Shine:
  Thirty Potent New Monologues for the Auditioning Actor
Two Minutes To Shine: Book II
Two Minutes To Shine: Book III
Two Minutes To Shine Book IV: Contemporary Monologues for Mixed Ages
Speak of The Ghost: In The Name of Emotion Literacy

Saving The World Solo

Pamela Sackett

Emotion Literacy Advocates™

Acknowledgements

Daniel Sackett*
Mark Magill*
Jennifer Johnson*
Gretchen Burger
D. Pablo Stanfield*
Dana Gold
Mary Beth Hughes*
Sue Ellen Katz

Georgene DeWald
Bonnie Tadej*
Rodger Scheibner
Bill Zama
House of Scheibner
Walsh Design

*ELA board member

Cover design and globe illustration: Mark Magill
Book design: Daniel Sackett
Earth photo courtesy of NASA. Other photos courtesy of the author's family archive.

Copyright © 2004 by Pamela Sackett. All rights reserved.
Printed in the United States of America. No part of this book may be used, reproduced or transmitted in any form or by any means whatsoever without written permission from the author, except in the case of brief quotations embodied in critical articles and reviews.
For information write:
Emotion Literacy Advocates™
PO Box 28002
Seattle, Washington 98118-1002
info@emolit.org
www.emolit.org

ISBN 0-929904-04-4
$16.95 US $21.95 Canada

Printed in the United States of America on recycled paper.

To my mother—a fiery and determined individual, to whom, as a child, I wanted to give a world of pleasure. Though I offered some buoyancy to her lot, I wanted and needed to give her so much more—an alternative world, one that had not been fraught with loss and suffering, a world that recognized her intrinsic beauty and worth, unequivocally, so that she could recognize it too.

To the ones of many.

Introduction

In May of 1997, I attended an evening of women's performance art entitled *Manifesting the Girl Hero* organized by my best friend and wise woman Gretchen Burger. One performance in particular grabbed my brain and my heart, shook my body with laughter and chills, and has left an indelible mark on me ever since. That performance was by Pamela Sackett, reading pieces of her latest work entitled *Saving the World Solo*.

I distinctly remember seeing this colorful woman take the stage, fabric swirling around her small frame, yet possessing maturity and wisdom that showed in her carriage, her silvery dark long hair, and her sweet bookish glasses. And then she began to speak: her distinctly non-west-coast rapidity moved at so many levels that I could only sit gape-jawed and listen to the magic pouring forth. As a lover of language, I was awed by her ability to manipulate and revel in words—to play with their multilayered meanings and their rhythm, to make them completely her own tools to express precise perceptions and nuanced tones of feeling. But beyond the word-dance, it was the content of the pieces that held me transfixed: Pamela Sackett was expressing the meta-mental and emotional process of the Strong Idealist who is burdened with a legacy of personal self-doubt and fear, living in a world that is structured at so many levels to foster and maintain that self-doubt and fear. As she expressed her dreams of a world filled with authentic, loving, *free* individuals, she simultaneously shared the enormous energy spent addressing her anxiety and scrutinizing all the potential ramifications of all the possible actions that might be taken in moving towards that ideal. Her monologues displayed in graphic high-relief the tension between being able to envision a world without inhibition and limitation, while living in a world full of obstacles that keep us from experiencing true freedom.

Pamela's *Saving The World Solo* reading was at once desperately tragic and profoundly hopeful. She demonstrated great vulnerability and sincere bravery as she wove pieces of her life story around her conviction to reach for personal and planetary emotional health, in the midst of navigating her own deep wounds, and ours. I wondered how many other people in the audience felt like she was telling their stories out loud, articulating their own idealism and self-limitation.

I know I did. Having dedicated my life to "accountability," at all levels, working as a professional activist and as a personal activist, examining and rooting out my own patterns of limitation that interfere with my ability to be my strongest, most liberated self, Pamela's words were like a mirror reflecting my own greatest hopes and darkest secrets.

It became immediately clear to me that Pamela's richly textured work was just that—her Work, her Calling, her Reason For Being On This Earth. To use language to bear witness to where we are locked up as a society and as individuals, and to do so by using herself as the primary specimen under the microscope. In doing so, she gives us several gifts. First, the gift of naming and shaping our greatest potential: the freedom to be emotionally authentic. Second, the gift of exposing the greatest obstacle to that freedom: our fear of vulnerability in being emotionally authentic, and the lengths we will go, because of that fear, to avoid our own authenticity and freedom. Finally, she shows us a path to our greatest potential: to examine the fear and learn the forms it takes; to then listen to the still voice inside that is already authentic and free; and to amplify that voice by sharing it.

Saving the World Solo is just one of the ways Pamela Sackett has been paving the path for herself, and accordingly for all of us, to realize our potential. Pamela is the founder of Emotion Literacy Advocates (ELA), a nonprofit community service that creates learning forums for insight into emotion through language and the arts. ELA is a vehicle for children and adults to learn to understand emotion, a critical skill needed to effectively and honestly communicate with one's self and others. Through thought-provoking art, including books, graphics, theatrical scripts, public events, web presence and recorded media, ELA offers catalysts for thinking in new ways—communication tools that can benefit whole communities by guiding individuals toward the kind of freedom required to be honest with and accountable to themselves and others.

    I am so thankful that Pamela decided to let ELA publish her 1997 creation, *Saving The World Solo*. Through language and personal example, her voice helps us access those hidden places of fear and hope, and in doing so, shows us a glimmer of how, with a little bit of courage, a lot of patience, and moving forward with deliberation and emotional honesty, we can indeed save our world.
—Dana Gold

Dana Gold is the Director of the Center on Corporations, Law & Society at Seattle University School of Law. Prior to joining Seattle University, Dana worked as Director of Operations and Staff Attorney for the Government Accountability Project (GAP), a national nonprofit organization that provides legal and advocacy assistance to whistleblowers—employees who report wrongdoing in the workplace. She is a longtime advocate for personal and institutional accountability.

Art is I, science is we.

—Claude Bernard

Saving The World Solo

First and Then

Frankly, I just don't know where to begin to save the world. Maybe if I could locate some small corner of it, some small problem, one that was manageable. But, if it was manageable then it wouldn't really be a problem and there's no point saving anything unless there is a problem, a substantial problem—one I could measure, one I could control. But if I could control it, would it be such a problem? I mean isn't the biggest problem the fact that things are out of control? How do you begin controlling things that are out of control? You've got to get some control of it before you get it under control. I need to find some *small* out of control part that I can control. You wouldn't blame me for wanting to control some small out of control part. I mean you wouldn't think I was a control freak or anything. I'm just trying to save the world.

And I've been trying to save it all along for as long as I can remember. First, as an infant actor, then as a child, then as a college drop-out songwriter, as a comedienne, a playwright, then as a game show question writer, then as a monologist…it was all so overwhelming—

until I saved the world as a griever-retriever in the lost land of feelings.

But you can't grieve and retrieve in the lost land of feelings as an upstanding citizen in the world of good-riddance, unless you call yourself a poet, and you can't save the world as a poet unless you make a career out of it, but everyone told me poetry doesn't sell unless you're famous, and I'm famous for rhyming in obscurity with no interest in a career in the sublime.

I tried to make a career out of educating people about the lost land of feelings...but not as a teacher. I tried to make a career out of guiding people into the lost land of feelings, via the emotions...but not as a therapist. I tried to catalyze people into locating the lost land through art, but not as an *art* therapist.

So, I tried to make a career as a rhyming town crier but tears get bad press, poetry doesn't sell, and the lost land of feelings isn't on the map, so I'm just stumped on how to get people to *think* favorably about feelings.

Most people don't even *think* about feelings or think about how they think about feelings or whether or not they think *favorably* about feelings, so they probably just try to control them—

—but you can't *have* feelings and control feelings at the same time, and if you can't have feelings, I mean *really* have them, you can't think favorably about them. If you can't think favorably about them, you can't have them. And if you can't have them, you'd *have* to control them. If you thought favorably about them, you wouldn't try to control them…

...unless you're an actor.

I started acting at the age of six days old when my mother hemorrhaged after delivering me and was returned to the hospital. Everybody was pretty freaked out about it but I just acted like I didn't care.

I think I had pretty good acting instincts as a newborn and I knew if I acted that way *someone* would hold me, so I acted like I had nothing to cry about. I think it worked. I think people held me. I've seen pictures of people holding me.

So, acting proved to be a pretty good deal. Every time something got out of control, I acted like I was fine and because my mother prayed to the God of Funny, I acted fine and Funny from 1951 to 1991.

And then I realized I needed to cry.

So I stopped acting in 1991 and started crying—for six years. *That's* when I landed in the lost land of feelings. My migraine headaches disappeared and that's when I began to think I could save the world.

The Problem At Random

The problem with saving the world is you can't just do it at random and expect to make a living out of it. So I went to a career counselor and she told me if I wanted to save the world, I'd better get an agent and the agent said I'd better get a publishing deal, and the editor said it isn't commercial so I went to a Quaker and he suggested I start a revolution or a non-profit organization or found a religion but I couldn't decide so I went back to the career counselor and she told me to go to a public relations firm and they told me to find a backer so I found a backer but she told me to help the children and I insisted we help the adults so they stop hurting the children so she went off on a ski trip and I went back to the career counselor and told her I still wanted to save the world so she told me to go to a therapist or take a nap or take out a loan...so I quit going to the career counselor.

Then I had an insight.

I realized I didn't want to save the world, I just wanted to give it a piece of my mind. But what if the world didn't want that piece? What if the world didn't recognize that *that* was precisely the piece, the very piece it needed to be saved? What if, somehow, I could get the world to recognize that I had the piece it was after? And what if the world took that piece and wanted more? And what if it wanted more after that, after that and after that? What if I wanted to keep a piece for myself and the world thought me selfish and negligent of my debt? What if I gave the world my last piece and the world returned it, unopened?

Too Much Fun

Once I thought I could save the world in prison. An arts education department for a local repertory theatre company thought I could so I agreed.

I read the prisoners some of my writings. They were captivated. I was delighted. Now here's a world I could save in a minute, I thought. They love my writing, they didn't want me to leave. Then *they* read something and I didn't want *them* to leave. We wrote and read and wrote and read to each other for two hours inside those walls. We wrote and read and wrote and read and drug counselors joined in. Word spread around the prison and the writing group began to grow. Everybody was getting along great. This is where it's at if you want to save the world!

Then, one of the prisoners left the room. Another one wanted me to leave. She didn't say so, but she kept staring at me like I was a criminal. Didn't she know I was trying to save the world? One of the prisoners wanted me to come back every day until he was out on parole. One of the prisoners wanted to move into my house. One of the prisoners wanted me to hire her as my assistant. One of the drug counselors wanted me to convince the head of the prison that she should bring me back or let me stay and the head of the prison thought everybody was just having too much fun to be rehabilitated.

Next time I think I can sign a contract to save the world, I'll think again.

I Wanted To But

I wanted to save the world today but I got too many phone calls.

I wanted to save the world today but I got a headache because I couldn't cry.

I wanted to save the world today but I had to make lunch first and that took up half the morning.

I wanted to save the world today but I think I had one too many frozen bananas this week.

I wanted to save the world today but my blood sugar is wreaking havoc.

I wanted to save the world today but I had an argument with this acquaintance of mine. I think it was something I said.

I wanted to save the world today but I'm beginning to wonder if the tendons in my knee are de-mineralizing. I think it was something I ate for 30 years.

I wanted to save the world today but I can't decide whether I should tell people I'm a woman who writes or a writer who acts or a person who cares or a Jewish girl who comes from the suburbs or a comedian who wants to be taken seriously or a playwright who writes books or a poet who writes monologues or a wife with no children or a daughter who's in exile or an emotion literacy advocate who invites people to invite tears.

I wanted to save the world today but I'm fed up with the Internet.

I wanted to save the world today but I'm tired of competing.

I wanted to save the world today but I'm missing a few degrees.

I wanted to save the world today but I've never gotten a Pulitzer.

I wanted to save the world today but my accountant moved to Slovakia.

I wanted to save the world today but I'm disorganized and I can't stop pulling my hair out.

I wanted to save the world today but I'm not on national news.

I wanted to save the world today but I'm afraid of flying, alcohol-based perfume and fabric softener.

I wanted to save the world today but I over-slept and now it's time for dinner.

Premature?

Once I thought I could save the world with a song but that was just too much pressure so I wrote a couple hundred of them and went to L.A. It was 1977. I took a small apartment near Sunset and La Brea and began to look around. I ran into an ex-playboy bunny from Massachusetts who was living with a phone systems executive who was paying her tuition at a Hollywood acting school. He donned blue leisure suits. She wore white leotards.

They came over to my apartment to listen to me play my guitar and sing. Kenny Rogers had just ordered a phone system. That was my *in*, he said. I played them another song and thought about saving the world through the cooperative graces of a white-haired Las Vegas act.

But I wound up in Tom Waits' agent's office—a curly-haired lawyer with a southwestern-style full liquor bar telling me I was ahead of my time and he couldn't deal with it. But the world has always needed saving—how could this pudgy guy with a knowing smile think me premature?

After two years of songwriter's business workshops in dark basement bars with red lighting, after recording music in the valley until two in the morning, cocaine up my nose, police helicopters overhead and a six-foot two-inch Dutch girl from the east coast harmonizing in my ear; after bar-hopping with a blond Adonis trying desperately to come out of the closet to his parents in Petaluma; after dating a two-timing bi-wannabe Jewish lawyer from Beverly Hills; after screaming to my mother on the phone, asking her if she was *trying* to kill me; after being woken up at four in the morning from a tidal wave in my head, I decided to board a different dream and head to where the world might be more amenable to being saved.

Addicted To Safe

All right, I admit it. I am addicted to saving the world but isn't that what it takes to be safe? I mean don't I have the right to be safe habitually? Wait a minute, do I have the right to be safe or do I have the right to *try* to be safe? If I have the right to be safe, someone is violating my right. Maybe I don't need to save the world, I just need to arrest it. And if *I* don't do it, who will? No, my astrologer told me not to take that tack—I've got to save the world because I want to, not because I'm a martyr.

I remember feeling safe once and then I pulled an ad from my mailbox selling me something totally unnecessary and bad for my health. So I thought about writing a letter to consumer rights—you know, to be safe. A call came in and someone else was trying to be safe by asking me for fifty dollars. I told him about the ad. He still wanted fifty dollars. Another call came in and someone wanted my old clothes and furniture. I told *her* about the ad.

Another call came in from a woman who wanted me to write protest letters. I told her about the letter I wanted to write about the ad. Another call came in and the same guy was trying to be safe for fifty dollars again. I told him about the ad. He chastised me for being redundant. Another call came in, no one was there. I threw down the ad and hung up the phone and crawled into bed and there was a racket down the street—a neighbor guy doing a drug deal. So I went to a neighborhood meeting and everyone showed up but the neighbor guy. We conspired with the police who conspired with his landlord to evict him. **But where's he going to go and who's going to replace him?!**

I crawled back into bed and heard the little boy across the street, singing by himself in the lost land of feelings—alone again in his father's truck, singing that lonely tune at the top of his lungs. That's it, I've got to save the world 24 hours a day or listen to that tune non-stop.

Rennie's Help

Once I followed a guru to save the world. I thought if I followed the guru, the guru would follow me and together we would save the world. Instead, I kissed his mother's feet in Houston, Texas, sometime in the fall of 1973.

I had been acting in Ann Arbor, Michigan. I played a street person in an educational film, had just finished playing the angry, tempestuous spirit, a portion of the spirit—the angry tempestuous portion of the priest's dead mother's spirit—in a staged adaptation of *The Exorcist* and was on my way to the Laundromat.

I noticed a flyer about a special seminar sponsored by Divine Light Mission. Their keynote speaker was Rennie Davis of the famed Chicago Seven. He was to be accompanied by a jazz guitarist by the name of Allan Thomas. I had been a student at Kent State University and fondly remembered Rennie's talk there about the killing of four students in 1970, one of whom I had repeatedly eaten celery with in fourth grade.

The hall where the seminar took place was stately and the

stage was draped in layer upon layer of ritual cloth atop which beamed a framed portrait of the boy guru. The next day, I spent hours at the Detroit ashram where Rennie and the guitarist took a special interest in my interest.

Two days later I managed to round up my portion of the damage deposit from a roommate, waved good-bye to the cinematographer of my debut educational film that I bowed out of seeing at the Ann Arbor film festival, stored my stuff at a former employer's, turned in a script for my first paid comedic role in a Charles Dickens public TV series, quit my job at The Bagel Factory and boarded a plane to Divine Light Mission's national headquarters in Denver.

It was snowing on my May 2nd initiation in Boulder, Colorado, where, thanks to a peach-robed east Indian Mahatma, I "saw the light" and "felt the vibration" but never did "taste the nectar." Still, I was determined to save the world with them.

Headquarters sent me to a dancer's ashram in Hartford where one of the dancers and I hit it off. It must have been those surrealistic winged, save-the-world heads I was drawing at the time. She emphatically identified with them. I emphatically identified with her. We began performing together. I wrote and sang devotional music and she danced interpretively to my songs. We defected to a chiropractor's ashram which put us on a circuit. Together, we committed song-and-dance prostrations from Iowa to the New York Father's Day parade to Plymouth Rock. From there, we boarded one of twelve buses for a twenty-six-city tour with the guru's brother, Bola ji, and his big band. We were scheduled to land at the Houston astrodome, where an ascension off this planet had been subliminally promised through the grapevine. We met the guru's family and their feet, flitted from booth-to-booth in the dome and patiently awaited lift off. At any moment, I was going to save the world with Divine Light Mission, my dancing partner and the toothy, blissed-out, ex-revolutionary Rennie Davis.

The astrodome didn't budge.

I called my father and he persuaded me to come home for Thanksgiving. I set up an altar in my room and my parents called me into theirs to watch an undercover reporter, on a talk show, expose the head-cracking practices—foisted upon disciples gone astray—carried out by an American disciple and the best friend of the very Mahatma who had initiated me in Boulder.

My altar disappeared without a trace and so did my hope for Rennie's help to save the world. My hope to do it myself waned for only as long as it took me to get back out of my father's house in Cleveland—en route to saving the world again. Solo.

Someone Told Me

I have to be honest if I want to save the world and to be honest, I really don't want to save the world but I don't know what else to do with it.

I tried ignoring the world once through smoke and powder and the world kept tripping me up with a fog.

I tried putting the world on hold but it kept popping up in the oddest places.

I tried swallowing the world but it kept throwing up all over me.

I tried living in a world of my own but someone kept borrowing it without asking.

I tried to make my world invisible but someone kept calling my name.

I was born to save the world. That's what my mother told me since the day she conceived me. Who was I to argue? It was a job for room and board and an occasional pat on the shoulder. I was born to save the world. My mother said so.

Someone told me my writing could save the world and then they left the country.

Someone told me my writing could save the world with a couple of back-up musicians.

Someone told me my writing could save the world if I'd write back in a little humor.

Someone told me my writing could save the world but I'd better put it in a screenplay.

Someone told me my writing *saved* the world and they put it in a letter. They put it in a letter that my writing saved the world.

Someone told me something I wrote allowed them to cry, allowed them to find the tears on the other side of an infant's laryngeal spasm, *their* spasm. Something I wrote tapped the tears they could never get to. Someone told me something I wrote allowed them to cry, allowed them to breathe the tears on the other side of an infant's laryngeal spasm.

Is this what my mother had in mind?

I tried shaking up the world with vigilant and radical confrontation but I was invited to shake somewhere else. I tried teaching the world but they put me in the cafeteria when the world was out to class. I tried administering to the world without a license and was summarily kicked to the back seat.

Where is your laryngeal spasm? I shouted from the back seat. Where is *your* spasm? I know you have one, to be honest, I know. Are you ignoring it, putting it on hold, swallowing it, living in your own, your own world that I can't get to to save?!

Don't disobey my mother.

A Little Longer

I planned on saving the world today but my husband and I aren't getting along. It's not that he doesn't want to save the world, he just doesn't want to make a big stink about it. I don't want to make a stink but I think a little confrontation is in order. He's not into confrontation so therefore I'm not so sure I can trust him to save the world. And if I can't trust *him* to save the world then who can I trust? I guess I'll just have to save the world all by myself.

We were doing a pretty good job of it together for a while there but then he up and decided that if he's going to save the world, he has to start doing it his own way which is fine but I don't think his way is going to work.

I mean I think he should do things his own way but he hasn't figured out what his way is exactly so how's he going to save the world if he hasn't figured that out, and as long as he hasn't figured it out, I just don't see why he can't do it *my* way a little longer. Maybe if we do it *my* way a little longer, the world will be saved and he won't have to figure anything out.

Now if I can just get his father to do it my way. If his father would do it my way, his siblings would and that goes for the rest of his family—aunts, uncles, cousins, nieces, nephews—and the whole way would spread like a healthy infection and eventually, my family would get the bug and if *my* family caught it, I'd get some time off from saving the world at long last. I mean if my family got it, I'd be home free—home free for the very first time.

I could handle a little change. I mean just because I saved the world all by myself as a child doesn't mean I can't get a little help now and then. Wouldn't that just be ironic if the help I got came from them?

If only my husband's help would hold out a little longer.

Loud and Clear

I went to an art gallery every week when I was small because I realized if I had to save the world, I'd better do some research, so I snuck out of the house and went there.

    I watched the people on the stairway and down the hall. I used the bathroom even when I didn't need to. I was trying to be thorough. I listened to conversations and took notes so I could save the world in detail. But

I couldn't hear what anyone was saying, I could only hear *how* they were saying it which was just as well because I didn't know how to spell.

    I sat in the gallery tea shop and looked at the menu. I couldn't read it but no one knew because I was a good actress. It seemed like everybody else was acting too. An orphan boy came in off the streets and asked a woman for a bite of her sandwich. She acted like he couldn't speak. I heard him loud and clear. He took a menu off the table and the cashier told him to put it back. The boy grabbed some sugar and ran out of the shop. I followed him back into the gallery. A guard grabbed him by the seat of his pants and hoisted him out into the alley. I ran after him as a fallen eyelash obscured my view. When I got there, the boy was gone.

How was I to save the world without him?

These Children

Two years ago, I read some poetry to kids in detention. If I thought it was adding insult to injury, I wouldn't have done it. But at the time, I thought my poetry was key.

I had written a book that unlocked parts of myself I never knew existed. I was enthralled and unspooked. I had summoned my ghosts, danced with them 'til dawn, and when the dust settled, my insight measured 20/20.

Never before had my words brought me to such a place. I liked this place. I needed this place. I wanted to inhabit this place with the whole wide world. It changed my neurons, my way of relating and cracked the code of emotion literacy—

to be in this place is to save the world.

Surely these boys in detention would see the light off these pages and be bathed by their glow. Surely these boys in detention would understand the power in tracking the source of original feeling. Surely they'd see the elegance of grieving and the strength of retrieving the ability to feel.

Surely they'd understand the gravity

                          in holding their parents accountable.

One day a boy wrote about his undying loyalty to a brutal father. Another day, a boy cackled and gave me the slip every time I called on his heart. There was a boy in the back—a natural-born leader. His writing made *myopia* sound like the Sermon on the Mount. Parenthood was a sacred image to behold as long as he was holed up in a prison and feelings were as expendable as these children.

The semantics of imprisonment crashed head-on. I pulled my poetry from the wreck and poised my pen for prose.

Together

I am going to stop trying to save the world. If I stop trying, I'll save it. I need to forget about saving the world. As soon as I forget, it'll come back to me. I know I know, somewhere I remember how to do this.

There's got to be a hidden trick, a cord you can pull that will unhinge a safety device. That's it—somewhere there's a cord attached to a safety device.

Years and years and years ago, someone planted a cord in a garden and it extends way down into the earth to some kind of safety device hooked onto a power source. If we could just find the garden that grows that cord and tug on it so the safety device is tripped so the power source will feel a little nudge, surely it will release whatever it is we need to save ourselves—just a little nudge, maybe a little nagging.

I know, I know, let's schedule a scream, let's scream for the cord in unison. Surely it will start to quiver, surely it will reveal itself. Surely it will send up a flare that will write a response with flames in the sky. We'll all hear it, together. We'll hear the flames whipping across the parchment sky. A satellite will send out a signal so the whole world can read the message on television and hear it on the radio and pick it up off the Internet. And those flames will spell out a message and the message will say:

"**Pipe down, what's all the racket? Dial the number of Pamela Sackett.**"

I promised myself I'd stay off the poetry. See what happens when you fall off the wagon? After I save the world, rhyming will be illegal.

To Be Chased

I forgot about saving the world one day and went to the park instead. There the trees were simple and kind—canopies over my head. I walked amidst the flowers amongst the grasses sweet and swaying—the world was glorious and beautiful there and apparently not in need of saving.

A man rode by on a bicycle, a harmless man or so he seemed. His son rode far behind him. I had not anticipated what I was about to see. A scrunched-up body struggling—little boy gasping to keep up with his father's pace.

"Come on let's go, we've one more lap!"

"One more lap?!" The boy's hopes were dashed for the promise of even a moment's reprieve. He pedaled, inch by inch by painstaking inch, in the direction of the man's relentless beckoning. Was I the only witness to this, the only one left there to do the reckoning?

A man with standards, a boy who couldn't measure up. That's one angle from which to view it. All I could see was a boy in fear of being left behind. And it seemed that what was there to see also was a father unimaginably blind. I wanted to catch them on their next loop around to inform the man of his son's state—in hopes of intercepting a pattern of neglect, preventing it's reoccurring fate.

And what of it, you might say, in the scheme of things, in the scheme of violence aflurry. What of it precisely, I say, let's catch such things as they fall in front of our eyes so early.

I go to the park where none are starving or beaten or brutalized, where saving the world efforts would seemingly be displaced. I would never choose to displace such efforts but for those efforts I seem to be chased. I have lost count of the many unseen faces I have witnessed in the park where children seemingly play in the light and their invisible feeling selves cringe to the depths, alone, in the dark.

Not Allowed

This book is not allowed to save the world. But after you read it, if you feel like saving the world, go ahead. Go ahead, save the world. Go on. Hurry up. Save the world. Do it. I dare you.

This book is not allowed to save the world. But after you read it, if you feel like saving the world yourself, go ahead, I don't care—just keep it out of my yard.

This book is not allowed to save the world. I don't expect this book to save the world. I expected my *last* book to save the world but I didn't want to sell it to strangers without seeing their resume first.

So I hid that book in the basement and figured if anybody wanted me to save the world with it, they'd fax me a resume.

It wasn't my idea to save the world with that book. Some woman whose mother was locked up for "narcissism" thought it was a great idea. She knew the meaning of emotional incest and wanted to see it in print. She offered me thousands of dollars to fill up my basement. I passed on the offer.

I read portions of my manuscript to strangers. They quivered with delight. They thanked me. They hugged me for championing their innermost feelings. They rushed the podium to purchase my manuscript. They rushed the podium to tell me to get it out there. They rushed the podium to tell me they knew a top executive at Harper Collins. I wrote him. The company sent the manuscript back untouched.

I called the woman who offered me thousands to fill up my basement. She doubled her offer.

Forty-five seconds after the truck driver unloaded my books and loaded the basement, I got a call from a Catholic university asking me to send them 45 copies. I got a call from a repertory theatre company asking me to read it to boys in detention, to men in prison to women rehabilitating. I got a call from a planning committee for an association of therapists. I got a call from a women's group, from a women's shelter, from a radio station, from a book store.

I didn't write that book to save the world. I wrote it to save my back. Now other backs came calling.

How many backs have to call to save the world with that book? How many backs have to be shown their backs to save their backs with that book? How many backs do I have to find to find backing for that book?

It's not the book, it's the message. It's not the message, it's the delivery. It's not the delivery, it's the application. It's not the application, it's the context. This book is not allowed to save the world until the world backs me up with contextual solidarity. Then the world will be saved without it.

The Right Questions

I'm running an ad in the paper about a special workshop. It's going to be a save-the-world workshop. I'm not going to tell people, at first, that they're going to save the world. I'll break it to them gently. It's not a lie—how many of you tell everybody everything all the time? If you tell everybody everything all the time, you'd never have time to save the world much less run a workshop.

How much time does it take to save the world? It takes more time than we're taking, obviously. That'll be one of the main lessons I teach in my special save-the-world workshop.

I have to charge for my workshop which is another reason I can't tell anyone that they're going to save the world. If they knew they were going to save the world, they'd charge *me* for it.

How many people do you have to save to save the world? Is rescuing the world the same as saving the world? What's the difference between a crisis and a tree falling in the forest? Which one is more expensive? Can one pay for the other? How can you tell if you've saved the world? *Should* you tell if you've saved it? What if you refuse to save the world? What if someone tells you you're not saving the world, you're just helping a few people? Will answering these questions take up too much time from saving the world? If we answer them first can we save the world later? Can we save the world if we have no answers? If we have no answers should we stop asking questions? That is precisely what I will teach in my special save-the-world workshop.

The *right* questions alone
can save the world.

I plan to breathe
during the workshop.

Anyone who comes in
breathing will win a prize.

For Chips

I got a letter from the world today telling me there's no chance in hell, I am without a doubt, don't you forget it, always remember, just remember, I am a chip off the old world.

This letter told me, in so many words, in no uncertain terms, I would be utterly speechless to do anything about the fact that I am a chip off the old world. "You are a chip off the old world," said that letter from the world.

I wrote the world back: "Come heaven or low water, hell or no water, I have no intention to save you. Don't worry about it. I'm not about to save you. Don't sweat it, I am not going to save you, old world."

I might, however, try to scream, I hope you don't mind, pardon me, but I have to scream it off its broken axis, never to be seen or heard from again, that is unless someone, anyone, would like to join me in reparation efforts to unbreak its axis, then maybe, just maybe, perhaps then, incidentally, you never know, one way or another, the old world just might, could possibly, any day now, if you please, oh please spin anew. Someone, anyone, like to join me in reparation efforts?

Anyone?

But, really, no really, don't worry about it, I'll just take my chip off, I mean I'll take my chip and go, just go, don't get up, really I'll see my way out, just thank you very much…

I'm ready now to dance to that old time rejection, that old time rejection that hurts so bad so much. Heaven help me, I cannot resist that old time rejection, that old familial touch. I didn't mean to rhyme there. I just couldn't resist the buffer. You wouldn't begrudge me a little buffer, would you? Or a little symbolism? It's not like I committed some incomprehensible abstraction or anything. I mean, you get it don't you? I'm a chip off the old world and I just can't stand it—oh my god, I'm a chip off the old world, I don't believe it. I've been bending over backwards for autonomy, you know, to be my own chip. This is really a blow, just to know, oh god, I'm sorry I am resorting to this rhyme, I have to face it this time without the buffer. I am a chip off the old world. I am a chip off the…but I know I've grown past the psychic height line of my great, great, great, great, great grandparents. I'm not going to mention the most recent of the tree here, especially not the main branch, the main most recent branch from which my chip directly sprang. Oh that branch, that chip bearer. Pardon my switch from long ago to not so long, from broad sweep to minutia, from passed past to recent past, from ever past saving. But I shan't despair—what's a little old world between worlds. Compost can be beautiful for chips.

A Better Crack

I was going to save the world today but my husband has gas and I'm afraid to leave him alone with it.

"What, *you* don't have gas?" he bellowed.

"*My* mother didn't die from it at age sixty-two."

"My mother didn't die from gas," he clipped.

"Take it easy," I cautioned. "You're going to give yourself gas."

It's just like him to ignore the symptomatic details. "Why wait for a crisis? Get yourself checked out."

"You want me to go to a doctor for gas?" he queried.

"Don't make a federal case out of it," I said, "just tell him about your childhood."

"Your childhood's worse than mine and your father died at *fifty*-two," he gloated.

"My father didn't die from gas," I insisted, "only the dog had gas in my family."

"And angels fly out of your butt," he contested. "Deal with your own gas!"

"I'm trying to help you," I pleaded. "Can't you see that?"

"There's nothing wrong with my gas," he self-advocated.

"I didn't say there was anything wrong with it. It's doing the best it can under the circumstances."

"What circumstances?" he quaked.

"Never mind. It's none of my business," I barked. "If you want to disavow your gas, don't let me stand in your way."

"Are you implying I'm not responsible for my own gas?" he rebuked.

"No I'm not, it's your father's fault."

"Are you suggesting I hold my father responsible for my gas?"

"If I can't inspire you to make a little change, to speak out to your father, how am I going to save the world?"

I was going to save the world today but my husband has digestive difficulties and I can't stop thinking about it. The minute he writes his father a letter, I'm going to take a better crack at saving the world.

Outside of the Inside

I went out of my mind once to save the world. It was 1975, it was nothing serious, it was all in the line of world-saving duty. I happened to know a transactional analyst in San Francisco and his dog. We met at a fern bar where they hung out. I was involved with a man who was twice my age. I met him at the same fern bar. Both men frequented the bar but not at the same time.

I'd drink brandy coffee *au laits* until my head drifted down onto the deck railing. I'd raise it for a sip and a snap. My boyfriend was a photographer and liked to snap pictures of me in the bar—it was the first time my thirst had a witness.

Between bouts, I'd return to the bar to see the analyst. He took one look at me and decided I needed to save the world elsewhere so he offered me one of his finest beds—

at San Francisco City Hospital's psychiatric unit.

I was the only one on the roster without a medication assignment. But of course, I couldn't have fulfilled my assignment to save the world with a medication assignment, so naturally, I was without one.

I proceeded to save the world, pill-free, on the rooftop with my guitar. It was a quiet saving—no fanfare—a subtle, basic saving on the rooftop for three weeks in duration. The Jewish family service paid my rent for three weeks on the outside while I was on the inside saving. They didn't realize this and I wasn't about to bring it to their attention. They might have thought me crazy to do it in three weeks. I knew I wasn't "crazy" or I'd be pumped with pills. Everybody in there but me was pumped with pills. Nothing new—I was outside of the inside, saving the world inside—just like home.

At the end of three weeks, I moved out of my apartment into a flat in Presidio Heights with a nurse who picked me up hitch-hiking. The world looked different without the rooftop but there was a cinema across the street and I could save the world in there, every afternoon, for two dollars.

Who says you have to be out of your mind on a rooftop to save the world?

When People Say

After I save the world, there will be some confusion at first because I am going to alter the entire language, that is to say I will incite a gargantuan semantical overhaul.

When people say they make lots of *profits*, they'll really mean they make eye-to-eye contact with everybody they see on the bus, in the streets and on the freeway and upon making that contact, they understand the roots of each individual's personality, including their own, what makes them tick, how different each individual is one from the other and yet how much the same and they'll really mean they feel a primal connection to themselves and every man, woman, child creature that walks the earth, swims the waters and flies the air.

When people say they are *successful*, they'll really mean they understand how to see through to the heart of every matter, no matter what the matter, and their communication to the heart is from the heart, for the heart, by the heart, taking all of the heart into full consideration, with the utmost of their conjunctive mind, first and before other more obvious matters.

When people say they *won*, they'll really mean they unfolded another layer of life within which they discovered a missing piece of themselves and that missing piece directly corresponded to the ones closest to them and how wonderful it is to know, beyond a shadow of a doubt, that all life has a connective pattern that reveals itself at every turn and that everybody *has* their turn...at the same time.

When people say they are the *best*, they'll really mean they resist competing with anyone *ever* because they know that all competing is really a divisive act cooked up by none other than those two feuding hemispheres of the brain who never did get along and are, nonetheless, perpetually in search of one another.

When people say they *love* you, they'll really mean they understand the nature of reflection and they claim full responsibility for their initial perception of themselves, through you, after which time they will be fully prepared, willing and able to be the object of *your* reflection, in kind, while bearing witness to any perceptions offered up by *post*-reflections, and will do everything within the realm of human possibility to see to it that all past, present and future projections standing between themselves and the other will be acknowledged, clarified and held forth as hard core evidence of a static force perpetuating the undifferentiated ego mass, ensuing forthwith, but *not* for very much longer.

When people say they are *bold, brave* and *beautiful*, they'll really mean they recognize the subtle, insidious ways they were taught to ignore their most tenderest of feelings, will rally their forces and champion each and every one of those feelings just exactly as a super hero would in gallantly freeing all, each and every one, enslaved by hunger, war and poverty.

Of course, I might have to come up with a little instruction booklet because I wouldn't expect people to know or even automatically default to these meanings, without a little guidance. Naturally, all sense of time, commercial practices and energetic output would have to be measured accordingly which would shift our sense of values which would take some doing. But, we wouldn't want to do too much on the first day after I save the world.

If all goes as intended, patience will remain a virtue.

Major Detail

I'm too shy to save the world. That's why I'm doing it telepathically. No paper work, no overhead, just simple saving, brain-to-brain, and I know it's working. I can't prove it or put it in a resume. I just know.

Of course, if I wanted to expand my efforts a bit, it could prove purposeful to avail myself of one or two or even three of the so-called concrete channels to save the world. I could tap the resource of talk and action for instance, perhaps put in a physical appearance now and then…how do I look? Do I look good enough to save the world? I mean, can you trust me to do it just by looking at me? I could find a stand in and do some ghost writing to save the world. No, that's just circuitous; if I'm going to save the world, I have to be direct.

Once I talk to save the world, do you think people will believe me? Will they get how committed I am by hearing my voice and seeing me stand before them? Will they write me off on appearance alone, and if I *am* alone will they think it's just too much for one person to handle? Will they think I'm saving the world because I have nothing better to do? Will I have to explain exactly how and why I am doing this to prove my sincerity? It's too hard to explain, they're just going to have to take my talk for it.

Of course, when people find out I'm selling the concept that joy is not the sole goal and that, actually, grieving your original losses is the key to individual saving and, ultimately, collective saving, the world will just probably run in the opposite direction.

And when they hear me say you have to overturn your whole thought process, stop standing on ceremony, question, confront and even boundary yourself from all disingenuous authority figures in your life, especially those that imposed themselves upon you from day one, they'll probably sue me for malsaving.

But you know, I have this feeling I'll start selling the concept and, just as anticipated, the concept will be flipped off and then, you watch, as soon as I stop selling it, people will start buying from someone else, someone famous, who flat-out stole my concept and converted it to a trend. And I'll just bet they'll get all the credit, money and glory but there's nothing I can do about *that* without trademarking "evolution."

Of course, being sincere about it, I don't care about getting the credit or the money or the glory, just so long as people start waking up. I don't need credit or money or glory. I can live off the satisfaction that people are coming home to themselves and each other and the world will be saved. And that'll be good, great, the world will be saved. Finished, done, saved and I don't have to give it another thought. That's probably how it's going to happen too so I can just stop thinking about it right now.

Yeah, well, after it's all over and the world is saved and someone, some *one* person, turns around and tells me, after the world is supposedly saved, that they can feel my pain, I'll have to take issue. I'll have to take it up with whoever did end up saving the world and let them know they left out one major detail—people are supposed to feel their own pain and feeling someone else's is an ignorant act of presumption and proof that the job is still mine—but only until self-empathy becomes the norm. Then I will graciously step down.

I don't know though. Going from that major percentage of the population that doesn't even have the word *psychological* in its vocabulary—going from *that* to self-empathy as the norm is going to take some doing.

Perhaps I could hire a few jugglers, a clown and maybe even a fire-eater, put together some entertainment package and turn it into a trend myself.

Of course, I wouldn't take credit for the core concepts *behind* the trend. I will admit this. I must give oceans of credit to Alice Miller. But I could say the way I apply her core concepts is totally and completely self-originated so when the glory, bucks and adulation for saving the world with a trend start rolling in, I can accept all of it with a clear conscience. I won't need it but I can accept it.

For Life

There's a group of Russian orphans that are being institutionalized with imbecile status whether they qualify for it or not and because of their status, staff pay is increased. Were they to be deemed normal, staff pay would decrease. Those orphans are not receiving any special treatment, training or care because of their imbecile status. In fact, they are being farmed out to old folks' homes and factories to work for no pay. This status will follow them into adulthood where they will not be entitled to vote, drive, own a home or make any decisions on their own behalf.

Some of them have not been spoken to or touched for seven years and are considered to be sub-human.

When these children are approached by researchers and child advocates, the people in charge abruptly dismiss the orphans, incredulous that such educated people would attempt to communicate with such imbeciles. The orphans are branded for life with no recourse.

Now what imbecile thought up *that* system?

I say we find the imbecile and ask the imbecile a few questions. Like:

Do you think flowers are stupid for seeding in a dumpsite?

Do you think that's any way to save the world?

If someone held out their arms and offered to hold you twenty-four hours a day, every day, seven days a week until you felt loved, appreciated and indispensable, do you think the dumpsite would turn into a garden?

It's times like these saving the world seems as likely as finding safe harbor in a war zone. But one of the orphans got out, spoke out, and tested out "normal."

It's a step.

The Real Ride

It all started when I wanted to fly. It didn't matter how and it didn't matter why. I just wanted to do it. I wanted to be harnessed, locked in and swaying with the pony-tailed, velvet-voiced, proud-talking, green-eyed and swanky, lanky Mary Livshun, our youth theatre company's Peter Pan—the director's favorite—next to his daughters, Tammy and Ellen, who were cast every year in the other two main flying roles of Michael and Wendy.

Oh! to be cast as one of the lost boys—it didn't matter which one as long as it was one of the ones who got to be airborne. At least one or two of them got to be airborne.

The director summoned me for a second read and my hopes went flying. This was it—my chance to leave gravity in the dust and commune with high altitudes of empty space on its own terms. Oh! to be one of the flyers, one of the few, one of the special travelers, one of the ground-free!

When the call came in, I was in the basement picturing the rip-roaring wind in my toes, made still by the news—I was to be cast as one of Tiger Lily's tribe, the irrevocably earth-bound.

Don't despair, I thought to myself. I didn't need to fly for the audience but fly for myself and, as a cast member, there was always goof-off time, hitch-hiking-the-harness time, time between official flying times when the unflown could get their due.

But there would be no possible due for me—not with a part too small to justify rehearsal-schlepping—only principal roles qualified for rehearsal-schlepping, my mother informed me.

If only I could reveal how principally I wanted this, but my eight-year old aspirations flew too low to be visible. If only I could have sent my aspirations flying past the eyes of the director, out of the hands of my mother, into the heart of my father who would have taken time off work just for the chance, *my* chance for a chance to fly.

So I watched Mary, Tammy and Ellen fly to their hearts' content another year. Penultimate pleasure eluding me, no gravity-snubbing harness protruding me, the real ride would come, I learned from my seat, not by saving a mere city or state.

Missing Ingredient

It's impossible, let's continue. It's impossible, let's get on with our day. It's impossible, let's continue. It's impossible, let's go. I never knew an accountant could help me save the world but that's what he said, over and over before he crossed the street to the parking lot. I didn't pay him for these words of wisdom, he gave them to me for free. *It's impossible, let's continue. It's impossible, let's get on with our day. It's impossible, let's continue. It's impossible, let's go.* It must have been all those years living on a commune with 137 people. This guy must be a master at group process, with a head for numbers to boot. Maybe *he* should save the world and *I* should move to a farm in Massachusetts. How can this guy be so profoundly existential and be able to figure out my tax returns at the same time? What made me think I could save the world before I knew these four sentences?

    I'm too short to save the world. This guy is six-foot, five. I don't know this kind of optimism, this kind of stamina. When I think it's impossible, I can hardly get out of bed. This guy thinks it's impossible and is raring to go. He must be crazy and that's just exactly the brand of human being destined to save the world. What made me think I could do it on anger alone? How could I have missed seeing this winning combination—righteous anger and crazy optimism? I can't believe I've been trying to save the world all this time without this missing ingredient. Who would have thought an accountant harbored the secret formula? I guess I don't need my pen anymore. Why write another word? I should just run down to the home center right now, buy a can of environmentally-friendly paint and blanket the city walls with these words. *It's impossible, let's continue. It's impossible, let's get on with our day.* If people could just read these words, they'd start saving the world themselves. *It's impossible, let's continue. It's impossible, let's go!*

If everybody would start saving the world, I wouldn't even *have* to get out of bed.

No one would be stuck with that subliminal resignation anymore, that resignation that keeps everybody recycling the same old garbage without realizing life just doesn't have to be that way. The world could be a truly creative place—everybody in tune, everybody working together with synchronous spontaneity, everybody fully capable of intimacy and the kind of open, trusting vulnerability that would cease to be associated with exploitation, everybody would be delighted by diversity and simultaneously in touch with the ultimate common link of authentic feeling, the world would pulsate with the kind of oneness that crusty old religions think you have to leave your body to attain, the physical and the spiritual and the mental and the emotional would come together and the full-spectrum of experience would be permitted to manifest ten-thousand fold and the rainbow of humanity could finally join together with all living creatures to unfold the miracle that is life.

My accountant is a genius. I'll never have to get out of bed again.

One Medium or Another

They left him for dead on the side of the road, sprawled out, skin coated with gravel, car over-turned—no college in the fall for *this* high school graduate. But wait, there was some movement, some breath, some redemption. He was in a coma for six weeks and when he awoke, his vision was blurred, neck fractured, speech garbled. Little did his doctors know this young man would grow into the finest comedy partner I ever had.

Portland, Oregon, 1979. Back from a European tour, hoisting myself from sleeper cab to cab, boat to boat, bus to train, trying to save the world from England to Israel, heartsick with nasal drip, on a dime. I was tending bar in a Greek restaurant on Burnside. On my way home, I stopped at a deli—he was holding court with his compatriot poets, sprang out of his chair and cried "Yiddisha momma!" I knew that meant he thought I'd eaten one too many olives, but I decided not to hold it against him for too long.

He was loved at the tavern where he read his "Brown Rice Poems" and recited Ginsberg by heart. I played him my music in hopes he'd help me save the world with it but we began writing comedy bits instead—I didn't want to be picky about it; I figured I would save the world one medium or another and was just ecstatic to have a partner.

Except for his diction, Mississippi drawl, and stiff neck he reminded me of Jerry Lewis and my childhood idol, Lenny Bruce—a man who, himself, made every attempt to save the world and failed. Perhaps he and I could alter tradition just a touch and joke the world into irrevocable salvation.

We met a gay priest who agreed to marry us in the delicatessen amongst the kaiser rolls and kreplach but we opted to begin our efforts saving the world posing as a poet and his lover in a bar—he doing his "I saw the best minds of my generation destroyed by madness, starving hysterical naked..." recitation, me—storming in through the back door—an irate girlfriend, accusatory, over-bearing, chastising him for wasting his time reciting poetry in a bar when he should be figuring out what he was going to do with his life. He pulled the want ads from his back pocket and declared he was going to be a doctor. "There are openings," he said, like a puppy in heat. The audience went wild. We were on our way.

I booked the act at colleges, galleries, secured radio interviews, stints on cable access and finally a comedy competition in a rock-and-roll hall. We were booed offstage for unreasonable expectations—we had unduly required thought before laughter and were exiled as inimical forces to the commerce of comedy.

I got us a booking to do a show in a theatre space where audiences were amenable to cognition. Nonetheless, I was starving myself and he was on a strict diet of zucchini, wine and Häagen-Dazs.® Not only couldn't I stand the disparity between menus, but I began to feel like a puppet. We had worked a couple of my songs into the act but as far as I was concerned, not nearly enough to save it, our relationship, or the world.

I returned to L.A. with every intention of saving the world, without him, in a juice bar at a celebrity health club. After two weeks, I returned to Portland, his beer breath and no bookings. Little did I know my saving the world efforts were en route to the greatest of heights.

We met his mother for cocktails at a fancy restaurant. When he excused himself to the men's room, she moved her chair in close, swore me to secrecy and proceeded to buy me off with one hundred and sixty-five dollars and a sickly smile. I promptly moved out of his apartment, he moved back with her to Las Vegas and I found a rooming house in northwest Portland where I commenced my search for another save the world partner.

I met him at a juice and candy bar. He was straightening out sesame chews on a display table and I was at the bar downing a liver flush. He lived in a hotel with a pair of sweat pants, an array of jewelry and a pleated Panama hat. His gaze was sexually transcendent—a man of few words—none of which resembled comedic banter so I rested assured my performing days had turned a corner and this man and I would be saving the world, together, in a brand new way.

His ways were mysterious, drip-drying daily in his sweatpants, after meticulous bathing, manipulating air waves with brass and steel palm-sized barbells, speaking reverently of the "Mother Ship." We extracted his belongings from a downtown hotel and he moved into my room at the rooming house.

He kept a close watch on me—regulating my sleep schedule, my sex schedule, my elimination schedule, my perspective, my whole life-saving life and my peanut butter sandwiches.

When he wasn't looking, when he was tucked into his trances, meditating on the "Mother Ship," I grabbed pen and paper and snuck up to the attic with my guitar where I kept myself from forgetting how to save the world solo.

He watched over me like an infant, taught me the secret art of enemas and rationed my Camel straights after blowing "psychic water" into the pack, converting smoke to a cooling vapor.

He stood on the bed, repeatedly, through the wee hours of the morning, arguing fervently with himself, pocket knife in his fist.

I grew impatient with his antics while the world waited patiently to be saved but my patience to save it could extend no further.

When I invited him to re-locate, he wrestled me down to the floor and began to draw the air out of my lungs.

How could he attempt to save the world this way?! How could he think it would advance our cause?!

He paused, long enough for me to exit his grasp, exit the room, exit the building, exit the street, exit the neighborhood, exit the notion that saving the world with this man was a brilliant notion—the notion of a novice in need of better schooling and much to learn about saving the world.

No One Knew

I was about to save the world Friday night but no one knew because of the storm. I tried to let everyone know I was about to save it but the wind blew my words in the wrong direction and everyone thought I was about to *shave* the world. So I told everyone what I was about to do, louder, and people thought I was about to shave the world with a vengeance so I spelled out, at the top of my lungs, what I was about to do and people covered their ears and held on to their hair with a vengeance.

Alive or Dead

A mere week after I decided to save the world with a book entitled *Saving The World Solo*, I got a call from a guy who was producing a show called *Ending The World En Masse*. My thinking went as follows: perhaps the contrast between saving and ending would be so powerful that a map to the lost land of feelings would be conjured alchemically and the world would neither be saved or ended but found.

"We want to assault the audience," he said. "I have no aspirations to become a social worker. I am demanding the end of humanity—no statement, no conscience, a multi-media thing with shills and shock, odd visuals and experimental music. You see, I have some footage left over of Hitler and the like and I want to do this reverse Nietzsche thing, mocking world governments, mirroring dictators, I want some loud poets, real loud, art for art's sake."

"Um, well, uh, um, where did you get the Hitler footage?"

"I got the footage to do a music video for my friend's band but my friend committed suicide. So I'm using it for this thing instead."

"Oh, I see." I said, seeing the lost land of feelings from his heart to his head. If only I were a master cartographer.

"My friend overdosed from heroin," the man said, "he and his band just signed a huge deal with MCA—I think he was celebrating too hard."

"*Celebrating?!*" I thought.

No grieving or retrieving for *this* man (or his friend). If I paid for his ticket to the lost land of feelings, begged and pleaded, offered to carry him there on my back, no charge, I doubt he'd quick start packing.

Alive or dead, he is in love with the end and saving the world obviously seems pointless to him, so might as well do something with no point in the city of numbness and despair.

"I got thousands of responses from poets chomping at the bit to join me with this ending the world show."

I thanked him for the call, wished him luck with it all and hung up the phone from there.

When I save the world, will world-ending producers make a deal to unsave it?

Through The Belly

I wanted to save the world in his eyes, in his arms, in his touch, I wanted to save the world like so—so, so very much—I wanted to save the world in his thoughts but those shots, but those shots, but those shots, but those shots, but those shots.

We were drifting after gifting and then bang! our sleep—forestalled. *Someone shot or someone shooting?* Adrenaline is indiscriminate, it shoots through veins, in an instant, from the sound of a prospect sickening.

"It's much better to drop to the floor and watch TV than curse the gunshots, we just don't look out the window that faces the street," she said "we leave our living room barren, if the shots get through, it's really OK, we've got a TV in the bedroom…"

I wanted to save the world, not a world in that direction; I wanted to save the world, not the world riddled with disaffection; I wanted to save the world not the shooting and the screaming, not the bound-up, blistered, bleeding; I wanted to save the world, not the blind to blind blind leadings, not the terrible, twisted treatings.

I wanted to save the world in his eyes, I wanted to save the world from the lies that this is the world, the world as it goes, this is the world so lay low and low and low and low and lower and low—

"We'd have been here sooner but the homicides are keeping us so busy, all our cases are prioritized. Homicides rate higher than random drive-by victimless shootings; it's just stupid kids with guns. They like to shoot them in the air but occasionally they miss the air and shoot each other…"

I wanted to save the world in his eyes, in his arms, in his touch, I wanted to save the world like so—so, so very much—I wanted to save the world in his thoughts but those shots…

"The neighbors are on top of this," she said. "We found twelve casings in the lawn, it was a 44 magnum, stolen, but why dwell on it when you can just as easily pick up the phone…"

I wanted to save the world but I can't call this one my own with wild horses galloping, blindly, through the belly of our home.

Frenzied Movement

"I have a hunch you're harboring a latent blast furnace," Professor McGore said as he invited all the actors to stay and watch me expand my audition into an improv solo. I called up a vivid memory of a bout with mescaline a few years back—circa 1970, Columbus, Ohio. I bent over from the waist and rose up slowly, a lit match in one hand held out like a torch, then waved it once to extinction. I stared into space as though reading the Akashic records, cocked my head to one side, thought about saving the world and launched into frenzied movement.

I was working at The Bagel Factory in Michigan. McGore walked in, informed me that he wrote a part into his movie because of that improv and offered it to me on the spot. Saving the world on celluloid was a technique I had yet to try, but I was determined to make a go of it.

They filmed me on Detroit Street reading the riot act to my multiple personalities while the movie's main characters passed me all agape. They shot the scene in forty-five minutes in front of a boarded up old building.

The movie won twelve awards. "They thought you were really crazy and we filmed you there by accident." He reiterated a number of rave reviews about my performance but obviously had no intention of saving the world with it.

McGore took his highly acclaimed doctoral thesis film to California and used it to finance a start-up movie company.

I saw him once again six years later in a hot shower in West Los Angeles but I never saw him again after that which was fine with me. Why bother pretending to save the world on film or in the flesh when I could do it for real in my mind.

Get It Done

I was walking down the street in a state of total and utter perplexity, feeling incompetent, ashamed, baffled. Why can't I do it? Why can't I just, you know, save it?

I have tried to forget, tried to distract myself with every dog and pony show under the sun but this job just follows me everywhere I go. I just can't lose it for the life of me.

So if it's my job, why can't I do it and be done with it? Saving the world can't be this hard. Saving the world can't be this outlandish.

All right, it's not hard, I'm just too stupid to pull it off. It's not outlandish, I'm the one that's out of it or I could get in there and get it done. How many years is it going to take? If I were really smart, I'd have done it already. What is tripping me up here? I must be missing something—some perspective on how to go about it so that it happens, so that the world gets saved already. Come on. What's the deal? What do I have to do? What do I have to figure out here to get this done?

"Toby! Come here, Toby! Now, Toby, you're too excited. Toby! Toby, if you are going to misbehave, if you're going to get too excited and misbehave, you're going on the leash. Come here, Toby. " (click)

It's fantastic isn't it? This world is just fantastic. You start spinning in perplexity on how to save it and what does this wonderful world of ours do? It stops me on a dime to hand me the answer.

And I thought I was stupid because I couldn't figure out how to save the world already and what does the world do? It sends me a dog and its mistress to spell it out in plain English.

If the world weren't so disobedient, I wouldn't have to save it. If the world weren't so excited, I'd have my hands free. But the world is misbehaving and the world is just too excited so I can stop trying to save it right now and just head out to the nearest restraint supply house and get me the biggest bit and bungee cord on the market or better yet, steel cable and a couple of gigantic paper clips. *That'll* teach the world.

And I thought it was my own stupid fault. Preposterous!

More Approachable

I was going to save the world tonight but they wanted me to fill out a form first. In twenty words, they wanted me to say just exactly how I was going to do it. I have nothing against distillation but it's difficult to distill on command. And what if my essence isn't their essence? What if I spend eighteen hours trying to come up with CliffsNotes™, trying to come up with this form-fit abbreviation for saving the world and the form-readers end up using a different dictionary—a paltry twenty painstaking words defined this way instead of that and there'd be nothing in the world I could do about it.

I was going to save the world tonight, really, I was going to do it once and for all, but there was this form, this call for circumscription and I didn't want to answer that call. I didn't want to bear down on the complexity. I didn't want to skin it alive. I didn't want to skin it at all. Twenty words, my life-saving foot.

I'll save the world without this form, if it takes me all night to do it. I'll save the world—form-free. I'll save the world from forms. That's it!

I'll save the world from forms.

Could this be why it's taken me so long to save the world—because I was without a niche? It was all too big, overwhelming, insurmountable, wasn't it? How could I have ever tried to save the world without a niche, a manageable goal? That's why it's been so hard for me to save the world all along. I had to narrow the saving down, make it more approachable. Now I've got my approach. I will save the world from forms. Saving the world doesn't get any better than this. I have found the one thing that cannot be misinterpreted, ill-defined or co-opted, the one thing that will break through all barriers—simple, self-explanatory, terse. **I will save the world by removing all forms.** There! They can keep their measly twenty words—I did it in nine!

Always and Forever

I am composing a get saved card to the world, choosing my words very carefully as I am wont to do. Not to be monomaniacal or anything, but, as my words have always come to *my* aid, my words are bound to come to the aid of the world and get it wonderfully saved in no time.

Of course, I wouldn't want to place over-bearing expectations on my words. I wouldn't want to demand my words jump through hoops or anything. I wouldn't think of asking them to bend over backwards when they are designed to stand upwards on the page. I wouldn't want my words to think that it was all entirely up to them, but then, they do such a good job of it, one word leading to each other, lending to each other and flat-out giving carte blanche to each other.

They are just about asking I leave it up to them, just about, if not entirely. They are so capable, so willing and so unconditionally endless, how could I *not* think to depend on them for getting the world saved? And so of course I depend on them. I do,

I have and I always will. And, of course, the world will respond, in kind, to my words on the get saved card and I can consider it a done deal.

And the deal will be that everyone will see that all that was missing were the right words, at the right time, in the right order, and they never have to be missing again.

Of course, if the world does not get saved after I send this card, well, I just may have to panic for several years or perhaps take stock and do a little reorganization. That's all, just rearrange a few of my words maybe even, albeit regrettably, drop some of them out and if that doesn't do it, maybe, just maybe, I'll have to take a good long look at those words and double check if any of them got out of line when I wasn't looking.

But then, my words have always turned things right. Why in the name of verbal language would they all of a sudden willfully take a turn in the wrong direction?

It could be the card, the envelope, the stamp. I could send another card, stronger envelope, more interesting stamp. And then if the world doesn't get saved, I'll just take it up with the world because I could not believe for one second, that the very dots, lines and curves that have always and forever cradled my falls would be unfit to at least fling a rope to the world and reel it sufficiently in out of the desperately deep end.

Perhaps my words will have to sit on top of the world for a while so they can sink in enough to adequately soak to the core— we don't want to forget the core. Not that my words wouldn't work as well on a flesh wound but we all know the world is not suffering from a flesh wound at this time.

And so it is at this time, this very time, that I will complete my get saved card, send it, sit back for the soaking and watch the world get saved.

Nearly Totally

I feel like I could save the world today. Yep! Today I feel like I could save the world. That is one amazing statement for a girl who lived in a mall for eighteen years. For a girl who sucked her thumb behind newspapers way after thumb-sucking was fashionable. For a girl who gnawed holes in her teeth with pumpkin-colored bubble gum called *Big Wad*. For a girl who thought the world was flat and that it was a crime to have any fat and that TV, truly, was where it's at if you wanted to hang out with your parents, in lieu of their free radical specters, like there was no tomorrow.

I feel like I could save the world today, I wanna tell ya, today I feel like I could save the world.

That's one heck of a statement from a girl who hid in a pen for twenty-odd years, who partnered, monogamously, with her primal fears, who walked backwards onto the island of fire writing messages into an unbuoyant bottle.

I feel like I could do it and do it alone in the company of solos who'll answer the phone when I call. I feel like I could do it all with them.

I feel like I could save the world today because I'm beginning to see it saved like grass growing up through a cemetery crack, like I could carry it all on my back—with a back as broad as the universe, the world feels light as an apple and as reassuring as a kind old man's graciously open arms, as delightful as a seasoned woman who senses my charms, as sensual as a young girl glowing in the arms of her very own *joie de vivre*.

    I know I could save the world solo today, I feel burstingly, anecdotally, very seriously—oh and incidentally, did you read about the cow that liberated herself from a slaughterhouse, single-hoofedly?—very nearly totally and quite utterably alive!

Compensatory Heights

Drooling and cussing, he was a spunky next door neighbor, amongst neighbors in our psychologically Jewish ghetto where a baby tree grew, reticently, in our front lawn. He taught me to kiss and then he taught me to sit with 128 other people in 1972's massive takeover at the R.O.T.C. building on Kent State University's campus where world-saving efforts were intermittently fatal, illegal and unaccredited.

He ran a *tranquillity* business with his girlfriend in her dorm where he hung his overalls, as though no one would notice, and no one did except for recurrent customers like myself.

I wore pajama tops and patched jeans around campus, the dorms and *the pit*, where charismatic politicos did Mick Jagger impressions to a blasting juke box; I joined the hippies and dogs in a big lecture hall, where a certain sociology professor commenced his classes with "salutations all you narcs and feds out there" and I thought world saving looked a lot like a big orange pill and a really cute boy or two-for-one tablets in an empty bed.

    He pummeled the baby tree repeatedly with his baseball, as a mere young'n and my father doled out endless reprimands but he made up for it, in the end, by doling out discount downers to me, demonstrating the compensatory heights of calming the world solo.

She Met Me

She met me in the dorm elevator where my folk group reverberated Simon and Garfunkel through the shaft.

She met me in the dorm lobby with bra-less breasts under a tie-dyed T-shirt to negotiate me out of my group into her duo.

She met me on an off-campus stage with back-up vocals, Johnny Carson parodies and nightly applause.

She met me in the dorm room to coax my virgin self into the arms of a Marxist latent paranoid schizophrenic.

She met me at a high profile anti-war march.

She met me in a photo on the front page of the Columbus Dispatch.

She met me outside of every dropped class.

She met me to wave goodbye as my parents choked their pride and drove me up the coast to a "health" farm.

She met me that summer at a nightclub in New York city, in flight from the farm, half in the arms of a man who didn't mind my not being unpounded.

She met me back home, with a fan in her face, my disappointed parents convinced she was wrecking my fate.

She met me to say it's never too late to save the world.

Closely Coached

I'm going to open an aerobics studio to save the world. We are going to exercise the emotional body because all the other bodies are covered. The entire room will be padded and everyone will be assisted to design new feeling-permissive frameworks, special outfits and aerating procedures. Everyone who comes to the studio will go through an assessment process to see how often and in what ways their emotional body is currently being exercised, fed and generally taken care of.

In the event a studio patron's emotional body comes in frozen, the studio staff will notify the patron and a bath of warm thoughts will be drawn with steaming, verbal compresses applied skillfully, gently and gradually to every nook and cranny. Partial thaws will be recommended until the mental muscles are built to support a full-range of expression. Interactive expression *between* emotional bodies will be closely coached—no feeling-prohibitive mentalities allowed.

We will have an extensive re-orientation program for all emotional bodies and family members. The Re-Orient You and Yours Program will comprise a major portion of the activities at the studio and all patrons will be given a take-home kit with a lifetime warrantee applicable only to those who are ready, willing and able to add their emotional bodies to a moment-by-moment exercise routine, shopping list and special date book.

Of course, I will have to franchise the studio because emotional body support needs ubiquity or the world just wouldn't be saved.

What's Left

I got a letter from my old comedy partner informing me that he planned on saving the world in Europe. He said he was going to dump his full-time job as an orderly in an Alzheimer's unit, dump his plans to do free library lectures about old age, dirty diapers and the ultimate challenge of living to be ninety, dump his ill-deserved kvetch license, dump his clunker typewriter, dump his typo-rampant economy typist, dump his computer illiterate frustration with the modern world, dump his anticipatory angst about getting one of his novels published, dump his best old poetry, dump his resistance to the Great Law of Impermanence, the Apocalypse and its next of kin—the lost value of art—dump his hope that the world will outlast his writer's block, dump the wait for the inevitable pox to befall him and acquire some guts to live the vagrant lifestyle—"nobody fights for *less*," he attested.

He went on to say he planned on eating in soup kitchens in solidarity with the penniless, believing for years that equality is not found through wealth. He let me know, in no uncertain terms, that he had every righteous intention of smoking dope on the steps of Notre Dame Cathedral in a noble effort to dump his obscurity and come out as a role model hell-bent on demonstrating to the world the world-saving wonder of—

a need-reduction diet.

It was a turning point, he said. He reached his peak, found his true calling, thanks to an inspirational 1985 French video called *Vagabonde,* and he planned on dumping his VCR for a plane ticket.

I wrote him a pointed note to let him know, unequivocally, that dumpsites are at a real premium, suggested he consolidate by dumping himself out of his mother's condo in Vegas for his up-coming fiftieth birthday, renting his own apartment for at least a year and *then* seeing what's left to dump.

Remaining, as always, his world-saving pal, I mailed my note post-haste.

Inertia Alone

My agenda is this: save the world; get it over with. Why drag it out? There's only so much time in the day, so many days in the week, so many weeks in the month, so many months in the year and so many years in a lifetime, so why waste a lifetime getting the job done? I'm going to put my heads together, right now, come up with the comprehensive, five-year plan and set it in motion. Once it's set, the inertia alone will finish the job. When the job is finished, I, for one, will be happy to celebrate, ad nauseam.

And what a celebration that will be—everyone riding that invisible wave with both eyes open to everyone riding that invisible wave; everyone waking up every morning, noon and night, ready to pack the picnic basket of life with enough rest stops and relativity to go around until we are done going around and can settle down for a good long nap.

I, for one, will welcome a good long nap after having saved so hard so solo without a vacation.

And I won't need a music producer to organize a televised event because by the time I save the world, everyone will know that *daily* songs *are* events and holding hands is not for broadcast company shareholders.

I, for one, would like to think up a whole lot of other things I could do with my time. I can barely, though am eager to, imagine what I might do. But I know that the world will be wide open for an energetically new agenda.

I, for one, would like nothing more than to spend my energy traveling to other worlds. If any of those worlds need saving, I hope the brochure doesn't mince words. This way, I'll know exactly what I am or am not getting myself into and I can choose to expand my practice or sit back for a few years and relish the fruits of my domestic labor.

Immediate Plan

I thought I could save the world in Cincinnati. That was after I thought I could save it in Cleveland where I *thought* I was doing a pretty good job of it—driving around all hours with a new friend learning the practical applications of creative juxtaposition, abstract thought and how to unfamiliarize myself with family rules. I was growing my own in leaps and bounds but my father thought I was growing distant so late one night, in the heat of a family brawl I was destined to lose, he kicked me out of his house. I was twenty years old; it was 1971.

I loaded up my car—a shabby blue domestic number I bought for a hundred bucks from the son of our family doctor—an adequate vehicle for my immediate plan to save the world. I put the key in the ignition, headed to the Case Western Reserve University district and showed up, with a flat tire, on the doorstep of my old folk singing partner from eighth grade.

She was living with her psychiatric outpatient nudist boyfriend in an apartment filled with empty space, anti-establishment dissertations and unworn clothing. I slept amongst them and a couple of their friends on a lumpy mattress on the floor, dodging breasts and penises for six nights and seven days, diligently dreaming up my next move.

I called my Cincinnati-born first love and melted into his voice as he suggested I drive down so he could help me "get my head together." I unfolded a map I couldn't read, placed it on the passenger seat and aimed south.

When I arrived, my first love was primping for a date. I promptly reminded myself of my true calling to save the world solo in lieu of my false fetish to resurrect an idyllic romantic pathway.

After thirty-six hours, he handed me a scrap of paper with an address scrawled on it. "It's not too far away from here," he said. "Rent is only $35 a month. You can handle it." I felt a wave of mild gratitude coupled with an anvil in the pit of my stomach.

"Take care of yourself," he advised, "and see what you can do about that self-loathing—it's a menace." And he was off to his next date for the evening as I was off to a hollowed out nine-bedroom mansion filled with twenty-something males.

My room was on the top floor across from a dark-haired mechanic whose weekly exercise routine consisted of lowering himself onto my water bed through a trap door in the center of my ceiling after which he would fix, fiddle with and test-run his motorcycle in the living room. The kitchen was a bug resort and my resources were wearing thin.

Luckily, my mechanic housemate had fifteen extra Arby's two-for-one coupons. I solicited single roast beef eaters in the parking lot, kitten in my arms, many of whom agreed to purchase their sandwich with the coupon and discreetly hand me the other. Content to have the sesame buns, I fed the contents to my kitten.

I serendipitously bumped into an elementary school chum at the University of Cincinnati. We talked about "the level," a sacred place of communication, and kept each other company in an ad hoc save-the-world atmosphere. Her big, black Lab dog ate paper, unceremoniously, in the mansion's living room as my chum and I alternately gazed into each other's eyes through the ethers and giggled about the imposing chest of our third grade teacher.

When I ran out of funds, she snuck me into her dorm where a long-lost cousin snubbed me for being a college drop-out in exile from our home town. Little did I know my own cousin, my best friend in eleventh grade, would turn into one of the biggest anti-world savers on the planet. She was joined by a host of dorm residents who had me branded as an outside agitator and subsequently booted from the dorm.

I thanked them all, silently, for their rigorous mettle testing, waved a warm goodbye to my dog-loving friend and headed for the nearest anti-war protest/peace concert where saving the world became as easy as going horizontal under the Washington Monument with a guy named Larry who charmed the sandals off my feet, blew me a kiss and left me barefoot amidst the majestic buildings of our nation's capital, dressed to kill or save the world—whichever came first.

Moment One

An old woman came knocking on my door in a silk smock, a bag to match and carefully applied burnt orange lipstick. "Oh, you think you can save the world, do you?" She glared at my front door, knocking on it with gnarly fists. I stared at her through a side window and waited. "Ill teach you to save the world," she cackled. I continued to stare at her through the finger-smudged glass. "Oh I know all about that calling of yours but what about me or do you think the world is more important?!"

I opened the door and put my lips to the crack. "May I know your name?" I inquired peaceably.

"Never mind, I can see your hands are just too awfully full with saving the world."

"I was just finishing my dinner actually." I dislodged the rice and vegetables from behind my back molars and gulped.

"Dining with the world are we?"

I paused for another second to clear my throat of half-masticated food.

She darted down the stairs, muttering to herself, throwing her arms around so feverishly as to dislocate a shoulder, if she wasn't careful.

"Wait—I didn't catch your name or why you're here."

She paused on the bottom step, turned to me and said, "If you're so smart, Miss Smarty-Saver-of-the-World, you should know my name and my business."

"Please tell me, old woman, what is it you need?"

"Never mind, the world is more important."

"But I—"

"Don't trouble yourself."

"I'm at your service, really."

She paused as though reconsidering, looked back towards me and then reached down as though irritated by a snag in her blue-tinted hose. She froze for a second, looked at me, still bent from the waist, then rose up abruptly and began to speak.

"Riiiiiiiing!" my phone intervened. "Excuse me a moment, won't you?" I pleaded.

"Do I have a choice little Miss Fancy-All-the-Time-Too-Busy-to-Save-Anything-but-The-World?"

"Riiiiiiing!" I hesitated.

"Oh go ahead," she sputtered. "After all, it could be the world calling."

"No, it's all right," I said obligingly, "the world can wait."

"I can wait too," she boasted, "the world has nothing on me."

"That's all right. If it's really important, they'll call back or leave a message."

"Is that a fact?" she snorted, sucked her lip, blinked hard—the air thickened. I sustained my focus on her.

"Just wanted to see if you were home, that's all."

"Do you need anything at this moment?"

"What could I possibly, right now or ever, need from the likes of you?"

"You will let me know, won't you, should anything arise?"

"Don't count on it." Her withered face contorted this way and that as she faded into the evening fog.

When I save the world, needs will be a shameless asset from moment one, tools to instantly fill them an on-going dime a dozen and guilt an obsolete source of fuel.

Get Up

I am not in the mood to save the world solo. In fact, I think I've lost my motivation for it. Perhaps I should join an organization. That would pep me up a bit.

I could take a position, secure a role, find a spot—a little cozy cubicle amongst cubicles—nestle in with the warm bodies, circulate myself, check out the bulletin board, the lunch room and the gossip on a daily basis, set up some good, strong, safe, intimacy-free working relationships, fix some set routine and mingle to my heart's content.

I could attend all those week-end retreats with other department members, form some bonds, buy some bonds and get a good check-up what with all the medical coverage I'd be entitled to, from joining.

I could make a name for myself, work over time, go that extra mile for a good long, appreciable stretch, say eighteen or twenty years—just long enough to get me to the point of celebratory recognition. I'd have it all—company, kudos, a couple of great reasons to get up in the morning.

Yep! That would stir up some motivation for saving the world solo. But then, with all that steady work, mutual admirability and scintillating socialization, why bother?

Potential Misuse

I can't volunteer to save the world anymore so I am going to buy up the English language and rent it out for income. This is a two-pronged pursuit here—a sort of entrepreneurial *slash* save-the-world type business. The income I get off renting out the English language is the business part and the extensive rental application that people will have to fill out is the save-the-world part. If all goes well, I will be well compensated, for a change, for my profound and loyal services.

I think this is going to be a real winner when it comes to the income end of things because, well, the English language is used more than toilet paper. I won't have to exert myself in any way, shape or form to cultivate demand. But the rental application could substantially limit my income potential because not everyone will be eligible.

I can only rent to those who fulfill rental requirements. Otherwise, the saving the world part of my business will be null and void.

And so, those applicants who fling the English language about carelessly, without general concern or specific capability to comprehend the full, personally cumulative, communally systemic repercussions resultant from their word-for-word use of the English language will not be granted rental privileges.

Testing for this potential misuse of the language will be rigorously required as part of the application process:

A three-million, three-hundred and thirty-thousand word essay will be required from each applicant entitled either: "The English Language and Me: How I Came To Love, Honor and Use It Wisely" or "The English Language and Me: How I Came To Murder, Maim and Destroy My Feelings With It and The Feelings of Everyone I Talk To."

Regardless of which title is selected, meticulous attention to detail, context and terminology is strongly recommended.

Once the application is filled out and approved, terms will be gone over so that each applicant understands what is expected and agrees to comply with those expectations throughout the entire rental process which will go as follows:

- Itemized reports will have to be filled out on a moment-by-moment basis by none other than the applicant so that assessments can be made as to whether the applicant's use of the English language is serving the applicant as a bridge on the way to complete and total unadulteration.
- If complete and total unadulteration is not reached or, at least, approached, rental privileges of the English language will be revoked.
- In the event rental privileges are initially denied or ultimately withdrawn, a series of preparatory classes will

be offered, at a reasonable sum, so that applicants can re-apply. Encouragement to re-apply for rental of the English language will be handed out, at every turn, at no expense to the applicants.

- After a three-year trial rental period, out and out ownership of selected portions of the English language will be made available. Once complete and total alphabetical ownership is attained, maintained and ardently applied, saving the world will not be solo anymore.

Package Deal

It's my birthday this Sunday so I'm going to take the day off from saving the world and accept the world as is for a day. I can accept the world as is as long as I know it's temporary. I can kid myself for only so long but as long as it's not too long I can do a pretty good job of it. I'll kid my friends too and they'll be thrilled. They haven't seen me take a day off from saving the world, no matter whose birthday it's been. They'll be pleasantly shocked since they've all been trying to get me to stop saving the world all the time for some time.

Their advice has always been: "there's only so much time, so pick your struggles!" But I wanted a package deal, so I picked the world. This way, no struggle will be left out. I know what it's like to be left out and I wouldn't wish it on anything.

It's going to be pretty interesting spending my birthday not saving the world. It's going to take a good lot of effort, time and self-kidding to restrain myself from saving it. I'll have to restrain myself from anything that might remind me of just how unacceptable the world is as is.

I could distract myself with something out of this world. I've never saved anything out of this world, so, that could work. I could save something out of this world—just a little something—nothing too hefty—just enough to keep me kidding myself long enough to keep me from saving *this* world on my birthday.

Maybe I'll find something so unacceptable out of this world that the unacceptability of this world will pale to the point that taking a day off from saving the world on my birthday will be a piece of cake.

Through It All

The whole thing was a security problem. I'm sure of that now. All the time I've spent *writing* about saving the world instead of just going out and doing it. It was just a security problem. I've got my security problem taken care of now…at least I'm pretty sure I do. I'm thinking: yes, I have taken care of my security problem now that I know I can travel outside of my home—outside far enough to reach the world.

First things being first, I had to make sure I could get out of my neighborhood alive—past the drug deals, the gun shootings, the crack-smoking, the bottle breaking, the fireworks popping, the car-squealing, the boom-boxing. If I could get out of my neighborhood alive, I could most likely stay alive *outside* my neighborhood and staying alive is pretty much my primary objective. Of course, I could save the world posthumously, but, that wouldn't be my first choice.

My neighbor called to check in on me as soon as she saw all the problems drift down to my block. She's kind of taken me under her wing—let me know I can call her all hours. Even if her house appears dark, she reassured me she's actually up all night keeping watch, taking down license plate numbers, polishing her gun. I would have rather she hadn't mentioned the part about the gun because guns put a substantial crimp in my sense of security, but she made up for it by letting me know she was keeping me in mind through it all.

She has reassured me over and over again that if I report what I see in the neighborhood to the police, she will back me up with her own call to the police and solicit at least one other neighbor to do the same.

I ran into an off-duty cop the other night—he was extracting all the spare wood from a construction site behind our house for a neighbor lady in need of firewood. I asked him why the police hadn't been responding to my calls and he said, "Get used to it." I let him know I *was* used to it and he said, "no, I *mean* get used to it—those are paper calls and no cop will ever come to your neighborhood short of a class two felony, which means no homicide, no cop."

It's amazing how a simple conversation can challenge my sense of security.

But I will rise to that challenge by calling my neighbor and just the sound of her voice will lay all my insecurities to rest. I know she's there for me and, somehow, that's all I need to feel secure. And with that security, I will leave my house, my neighborhood and perhaps even the country to save the world.

And in case my security is challenged to the point of impairment while I'm away and for some reason my neighbor doesn't answer her phone, I will pack my strongest pen and a ream of paper just to tide me over until she does.

Worth Taking

I was anxious. I was bouncing off the walls. I was abandoning sentences in mid-air, over-producing tangents, riding whole paragraphs off cliffs until the heat rose up from my toes into my brain, a kajillion miles an hour, about to explode. I was trying to save the world, non-stop, but this time, I was actually, albeit equivocally, asking someone to help me

and I figured this woman, this brightly creative, truth-soaked compadre strolling by my side could weave her way through my oral flips and frenzy and figure it out.

"I take baby steps," she said. Yeah, I thought and I've been chasing my tail up into my head in giant leaps and bounds.

So, now it's time to take a look at the cumulative effects of my long-suffering actions—an unsaved world.

I finally got it! Not only have I been trying to save the world solo but I've been trying to save it in one fell swoop—trying to find the singular antidote, the whole ball of wax, the cut-the-mustard method whereby I could get it all done and get on with some semblance of an unburdened existence.

But no! I know in my heart of hearts that this woman was on to something—this baby step thing must be the only effective approach worth taking.

She was calm when she imparted this knowledge—perfectly calm. Her words were full, sentences structured and enviably complete. Yep, yep, this baby step thing must be the answer. Never mind such a pace will take my efforts well into the next millennium, bogging down any hope for time left over to pursue some other, less cumbersome dream. Of course, two baby-steppers could probably cover more ground more quickly and there is no telling how much ground twenty or even two-hundred or two-thousand or three thousand or four million baby-steppers could cover. If only I could organize myself to organize others, I might just get the job done before they carry me off to the home. This way, they won't have to hoist the job in with me.

We sat down on a park bench, this beautiful, knowing, patient woman and me. I was wishing I could apply her wisdom instantly and begin taking baby steps on the spot by asking her, just her, if she'd like to join me in taking baby steps to save the world. But I was afraid if she said yes, I'd take leave of my newly-informed senses and in all my excitement, ask her if she had a whole lot of other baby-stepping friends we could ask immediately, if not sooner. I was embarrassed by the prospect, afraid she might think me unreceptive to her wise counsel.

So I asked her if she'd like to meet with me again some time, down the road, for a few moments. She said yes, she would definitely arrange to see me within the next two weeks.

I smiled, a baby fraction, very slowly, just to prove her effort to guide me had not fallen on deaf lips.

Index of Titles

A Better Crack 63	No One Knew 97
A Little Longer 37	Not Allowed 54
Addicted To Safe 26	One Medium Or Another 90
Alive Or Dead 98	Outside Of The Inside 65
Always And Forever 112	Package Deal 147
Closely Coached 123	Potential Misuse 142
Compensatory Heights 119	Premature? 24
First And Then 3	Rennie's Help 28
For Chips 60	She Met Me 121
For Life 82	Someone Told Me 33
Frenzied Movement 104	The Problem At Random 16
Get It Done 106	The Real Ride 84
Get Up 140	The Right Questions 57
I Wanted To But 21	These Children 43
Immediate Plan 131	Through It All 150
Inertia Alone 129	Through The Belly 101
Loud And Clear 40	To Be Chased 51
Major Detail 77	Together 49
Missing Ingredient 87	Too Much Fun 19
Moment One 136	What's Left 125
More Approachable 109	When People Say 69
Nearly Totally 116	Worth Taking 154

163

Pamela Sackett is an international performer, playwright and teaching artist. Founder and Artistic Director of Emotion Literacy Advocates,™ she presents expressive art and facilitates workshops and community dialogue through arts events, learning institutions, social service agencies, special interest gatherings and media outlets.

For more information on Pamela's emotion literacy work, booking an appearance or product availability, contact info@emolit.org.

Emotion Literacy Advocates™ (ELA) is a nonprofit 501(c)3 organization comprised of a group of generative artists and social activists in Seattle who came together at the turn of the millennium to further ELA's mission: to create learning forums for insight into emotion through language and the arts.

Emotion Literacy Advocates™ provides inspiring products to support your journey of learning and understanding.

ELSOTA! **(Emotion Literacy School ON THE AIR)** is a series of four-to-five minute radio vignettes designed to engage, inform and inspire listeners to discover new ways of thinking, talking about and viewing emotion. The first five episodes of *ELSOTA!* are available on compact disk, complete with a sixteen-page study guide insert.

ELSOTA! provides entertaining and concrete situations to:

- inspire thought, group discussion and insight
- model self-awareness and authenticity
- show the value of knowing feelings
- encourage responsible actions in high-pressure situations

"*ELSOTA! is a wonderful, innovative tool…Emotion Literacy Advocates has created a fun, creative way for teachers to talk with students about their feelings. There is application in social/emotional health subjects as well as substance use prevention, family life and relationships, injury prevention and safety, disease prevention and control.*"
—Lisa Love, health education specialist for Seattle Public Schools

For information on how to join the list of radio stations who have used *ELSOTA!* vignettes for lively public affairs programming or for underwriting opportunities in support of our emotion literacy awareness campaign, contact ELA at info@emolit.org. Visit our web site at www.emolit.org to hear a short excerpt.

Trigger of Light

Trigger of Light is an audio play made up of monologues, scenes and narrative that grew out of Pamela Sackett's work in King County Youth Detention Facility in Washington state, sponsored by Seattle Repertory Theatre's Outreach and Education program. Detainees' writings and verbatim excerpts from interviews with adults who affect their lives make up most of this collage of voices. The result is a poignant, thought-provoking and affecting story with an emotion literacy perspective and a glimmer of hope for change. Audio play approximate time: 32:30; radio interview: 32:00. The script for *Trigger of Light* with supporting materials is available in electronic form.

detention youth art

> "I think a lot about my brother who has been in prison for eight years for murder. He is really angry and violent. He is in much pain. He was never heard...he just needs to be heard... I saw and heard my brother and myself in these kids. I heard my mother in the adult characters. We all need help. I am happy to have had this experience. I cried—I feel my love for myself—I feel my pain—thank you."
>
> —T. L., audience member, Seattle Repertory Theatre

> "I found your art to be very understanding! I too wish to be able to come forth and speak of my angers.... My family is inclose [sic] with our inner feelings. Seems to come out only when something dramatic appears. I wish to speak freely about my feelings towards my family. As you know it's hardest to speak to people you love the most. Sorry time to go. I wish you the best of luck on your program and please continue. We need people who want to understand us."
>
> —T. H. D., Hall #9

Speak of the Ghost: In The Name of Emotion Literacy

Speak of the Ghost is an evocative work that taps deeper instincts and fleshes out, in a series of seventy-eight finely detailed narrative poems, the author's retrieval of a full spectrum of feeling in the face of personal and universal repression and censorship. Sackett's premise: "The greatest gift to be had in tracking childhood and teenage mistreatment is in developing the capacity to communicate with, be nourished by and house the great spirit in your own emotions."

Speak of the Ghost audio CD

In 1993, before publication of *Speak of the Ghost: In The Name of Emotion Literacy,* Pamela Sackett recorded thirteen of the pieces at Jack Straw studios in Seattle. Now you can hear the author in her inimitable, heartfelt style, still fresh from the generative process that gave her a deeper self-knowledge and lead her to the founding of Emotion Literacy Advocates™. (Running time: 42:52)

> "As I listened to you, I heard the truth of my own story, uttered with such passion and wit…I felt shivers as the wave of realization rippled through me. Thank you for putting words to my experiences. I feel more deeply empowered to utter my own story now."
> —audience member, Elliott Bay Book Company

> "Take a look at Pamela's book and you will find everyone on trial, caught and transformed. I loved those poems."
> —Arnold Mindell, Ph.D., author of *The Leader as Martial Artist*

Order Form

Emotion Literacy Advocates™

	Quantity		Total
Saving the World Solo	_____	@ $16.95 US =	_____

ELSOTA! (Emotion Literacy School On The Air) compact disc & study guide insert

_____   @ $30.00 US =   _____

Speak of the Ghost: In The Name of Emotion Literacy

_____   @ $15.95 US =   _____

Speak of the Ghost audio CD   _____   @ $15.00 US =   _____

Trigger of Light available on a suggested donation* basis (tax deductible)

   audio play & radio interview   _____   @ $15.00* US =   _____

   script & documentation (electronic) _____   @ $10.00* US =   _____

Sales Tax (Washington state residents only)   _____

Postage & Handling: US/Canada:

$3.00 for the first item, plus $1.00 for each additional item   =   _____

Total: _____

Ship to:

Name _____

Address _____

City, State & Zip _____

Phone _____ Email _____

Please send the full amount in check or money order to:

   Emotion Literacy Advocates™ PO Box 28002, Seattle, WA 98118-1002

Order by credit card at **www.emolit.org** and find out what's new. Thank you!

(Pamela Sackett's *Two Minutes To Shine* series is available through Samuel French, New York.)